An invaluable

COMP[LETE]
TRIP
DIARY

A day-by-day diary of your vacation

Easy-to-use vacation budget planner

Helps organize your trip for more fun

Keep your schedules, plans, and vital
information at your fingertips

Names, addresses, important dates

*An indispensable planner, organizer, record
and guide for you to use before, during
and after your trip or vacation*

An invaluable travel companion

COMPLETE
TRIP
DIARY

Write down, record,
explore—and remember!

COMPLETE TRIP DIARY

Copyright 1994 by
Marlor Press, Inc.

ISBN 0-943400-78-3
Revised Edition

10 9 8 7 6 5 4 3 2 1
Manufactured in the United States of America

Distributed to the book trade by
Contemporary Books, Inc., Chicago, Illinois

MARLOR PRESS, INC.
4304 Brigadoon Drive
Saint Paul, MN 55126

CONTENTS

THE
COMPLETE
TRIP DIARY

...can make your vacation or trip more memorable and fun. As a day-by-day diary, it can become a terrific record and memento of your vacation. As a planner, it can help organize your plans and let you make the most of your time. Financially, it can be a great help!

The *Complete Trip Diary* is divided into three parts:

1/ Before you leave
2/ During your vacation
3/ Memories of my trip

1. Before you leave. Here's a handy place to make plans, keep notes, and write down things to do. A *Budget Planner* lets you figure how much money you want to spend---to maintain control of your funds.

2/ During your vacation. You'll want to keep a journal of the highlights of the day. Each two-page unit contains, in addition to the diary, a personal planner and schedule organized around a single day's activities. Here, too, is a handy day-by-day budget record. This can help you keep track of your costs and let you better control your budget. (Never run short of money again!)

3/ Memories of my trip. This is a place to paste in small mementoes of your trip that can bring back warm memories for years to come.

Part One

BEFORE

YOU

LEAVE

Vacation checklist

My list of things to do

My budget planner

Schedule

My personal record

Emergency information

Getting
ready
to go

There are many things to do to get ready for a trip. It's important that you begin your preparations well in advance and do a little bit regularly over a period of time. In that way, you'll save yourself a lot of last-minute rush. You'll also get your vacation off to a better start.

If you're traveling with your family, getting ready to go should also involve them. Planning together can help all of you prepare for your trip and enjoy it more.

Vacation checklist

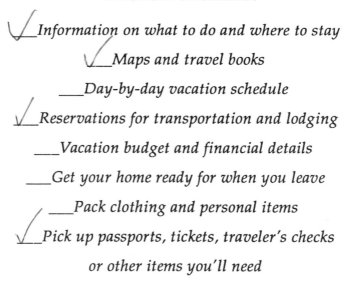

___Information on what to do and where to stay

___Maps and travel books

___Day-by-day vacation schedule

___Reservations for transportation and lodging

___Vacation budget and financial details

___Get your home ready for when you leave

___Pack clothing and personal items

___Pick up passports, tickets, traveler's checks
or other items you'll need

My list
of things
TO DO
before I go

1/ Clean apartment
2/ Pack
3/ stop at cleaners
4/ pick up cleaning
5/ get stock up items *too apartment*
6/ get beauty and items *Jmk*
7/ make instructions for
8/ go to mall for last minute *things*
9/ get money out of Bank *to*
10/ iron all clothes
11/
12/
13/
14/
15/
16/
17/
18/

19/ _____

20/ _____

21/ _____

22/ _____

23/ _____

24/ _____

25/ _____

26/ _____

27/ _____

28/ _____

29/ _____

30/ _____

31/ _____

32/ _____

33/ _____

34/ _____

35/ _____

36/ _____

37/ _____

38/ _____

39/ _____

40/ _____

*As long as you keep your sense of
humor, you're ahead of the game.*

$ $ $ $ $
My daily
Budget Planner

(Use this to plan your day-by-day cash disbursements)

Number of days of trip 4 weeks

1/ Lodging budget per day	$_____
2/ Food budget	
Breakfast	$_____
Lunch	_____
Dinner	_____
Snacks	_____
Total	$_____
3/ Daily transportation	$_____
4/ Other costs	$_____
5/ Entertainment	$_____
6/ Shopping	$_____
Total per day	$_____

7/ Enter your **Total per day** in the budget section of each of the **Diary Pages.**

8/ Overall Daily Trip Budget $_____
(Multiply your Total Per Day Budget times the number of days you will be on vacation to give you your Overall Daily Trip Budget.)

Personal record

My name __CHRISTine Konopczyk__
City __N. Wales__ State __PA__ Zip __19 454__
Home telephone (__215__) __855 - 4928__
Office telephone (__610__) __995 - 0202__

Height __5-6"__ Weight __150__

Age __30__ Religion __—__

In case of emergency, please contact

1/ Name __Robert Foote__
City __mT. Top__ State __PA__ Zip __18707__
Home telephone (__717__) __678 - 3823__
Office telephone (__800__) __233 - 8373__
Instructions: _____

2/ Name __Tom Konopczyk__
City __Telford__ State __PA__ Zip __18969__
Home telephone (__215__) __721 - 9447__
Office telephone (__215__) __646 - 7460__
Instructions: _____

My home physician or clinic:

Name _____

City _____ State _____ Zip _____

Office telephone (_____) _____

Emergency telephone (_____) _____

My special medical needs or instructions

_____

_____

_____

_____

Other members of my party

_Monique___Foote_____

_____

_____

_____

_____

_____

Special instructions in case of emergency

_____

_____

_____

_____

Notes

----

*Travel with a positive outlook. A lot
depends on how you look at things.*

Part Two

DURING

YOUR

VACATION

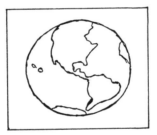

Items to remember

Automobile record

How to use your daily diary & planner

Daily diary & planner pages

Trip notes

Items to remember

Schedule & events:

Time	Date	Item

1/ _____

2/ _____

3/ _____

4/ _____

5/ _____

6/ _____

7/ _____

8/ _____

9/ _____

10/ _____

11/ _____

12/ _____

13/ _____

14/ _____

15/ _____

16/ _____

17/ _____

18/ _____

People, addresses & telephone numbers

_____

_____

_____

_____

_____

_____

_____

_____

_____

Travel check numbers:

_____

_____

_____

_____

Other items:

_____

_____

_____

Tolerance is sometimes more impor-
tant than knowledge.

Automobile record

Mileage & gasoline analysis:

Date	Gallons	Cost	Miles	Miles per gallons
Total	Gallons	Cost	Miles	Miles per gallon

Automotive services, repairs & other expenditures:

Date	Item	Cost
1/		
2/		
3/		
4/		
5/		
6/		
7/		
8/		
9/		
10/		
11/		
12/		

Total Cost _____

Other automobile costs:

1/		
2/		
3/		
4/		

Total Cost _____

How to use your diary and daily planner

Each of the two-page units is geared for a single day's vacation activities. Here you can write your journal, plan your vacation, organize your schedules, keep a "to do" list, and keep control of your money.

The daily pages are divided into **eight** segments: **1/** Trip Day **2/** Today **3/** Today's checklist **4/** My schedule **5/** Today's diary **6/** What I spent today **7/** Picture record and **8/** Names, addresses & places to remember

1/ Trip Day: This column of figures across the top of the page indicates the vacation length and day of vacation. Put an X for the total days of vacation. Circle the number for today's vacation day.

2/ Today: Here you can fill in today's **Date.** Below that, **Your Location,** which can be a city, area, your hotel, or enroute. And, lastly, jot down a few words about the **Weather.**

3/ Today's checklist: Here's a handy place to write down the things you want to be certain to remember or notes to jog your memory. For example, you can write down: Purchase tickets for evening. Or, buy film.

4/ My schedule: You can organize your day by jotting down what you have actually planned for each day, including times and places. Or, if you want to <u>plan</u> a day, write in times and places so you have a target schedule.

5/ Today's diary: This is your personal journal of your trip. Facts, ideas, impressions. It's not hard to do and shouldn't take more than a few minutes a day. Set a time to do this every day, such as dashing off a few words at dinner or at the end of the day.

Your journey can give you inspiration. You can describe things around you in a chronological fashion, jotting down what you actually did as you did it. Perhaps you can refer to a map or brochure. Give your journal a feeling for where you are, what you are doing, and most important, what you experience. Journaling is important and you can grow with your journal.

6/ What I spent today: Here is your all-important budget record and planner. At the top right of the box is your **Target budget today,** which you filled in from your pre-vacation budget planning (Part 1). This is your target figure to spend today. As you spend daily, write in the amounts.

At the end of the day, add up your **Total spent today.** Then figure the amount over, or under, your planned daily budget. If you've got a surplus, or a deficit, move that amount forward to tomorrow's **Target budget today.**

7/ Picture record: Keep a record of the photographs you took, of who, what or when.

8/ Names, addresses & places to remember: Record the names, addresses and telephone numbers of new friends.

Remember

Just a few words each day can help you get more out of your trip. And, when your journey is over, your **Complete Trip Diary** will be a treasury of memories that you can keep on your library shelf.

A stranger today, a friend tomorrow.

Today's checklist

1/ _____
2/ _____
3/ _____
4/ _____

TODAY

Date

Location

Weather

TODAY'S DIARY

What I spent today

Target budget today:
$_____

Food
  Breakfast $_____
  Lunch   _____
  Dinner   _____
  Snacks   _____
Food Total $_____

Entertainment $_____

Shopping $_____

Lodging $_____
Transportation $_____

Other $_____
Total spent today $_____
  Over/under budget: $_____

My schedule today:

1/ _____

2/ _____

3/ _____

4/ _____

- -

- -

- -

- -

- -

- -

- -

- -

Picture record
Pix #   *Description*

Names, addresses
and places to remember

Today's thought

*A journey of a thousand miles
begins with a single step.*

Today's checklist

TODAY

1/ _____

2/ _____

Date

3/ _____

Location

4/ _____

Weather

TODAY'S DIARY

What I spent today ☆   *Target budget today:*

$_____

Food
   Breakfast $_____   Entertainment $_____
   Lunch   _____
   Dinner   _____
   Snacks   _____   Shopping $_____
Food Total $_____

Other $_____

Lodging $_____   Total spent today $_____
Transportation $_____   *Over/under budget:* $_____

13 14 15 16 17 18 19 20 21 22 23 24 25 26 27 28

My schedule today:

1/ _____

2/ _____

3/ _____

4/ _____

☆

- -

- -

- -

- -

- -

- -

- -

- -

- -

- -

Picture record
Pix #   *Description*

_____

_____

_____

_____

_____

_____

_____

Names, addresses ☆
and places to remember

_____

_____

_____

_____

Today's thought

One is not born a traveler. One becomes one.

Today's checklist

1/_____

2/_____

3/_____

4/_____

TODAY

Date

Location

Weather

TODAY'S DIARY

What I spent today

Target budget today:
$_____

Food

Breakfast $_____
Lunch   _____
Dinner   _____
Snacks   _____
Food Total $_____

Entertainment $_____

Shopping $_____

Lodging $_____
Transportation $_____

Other $_____
Total spent today $_____
Over/under budget: $_____

13 14 15 16 17 18 19 20 21 22 23 24 25 26 27 28

My schedule today:

1/ _____

2/ _____

3/ _____

4/ _____

☆

- -

- -

- -

- -

- -

- -

- -

- -

- -

Picture record

Pix #   *Description*

_____

_____

_____

_____

_____

_____

_____

Names, addresses
and places to remember

_____

_____

_____

Today's thought

*Your vision improves when you stand
on tiptoes.*

TODAY ☆

Today's checklist

1/ _____

2/ _____

3/ _____

4/ _____

Date

Location

Weather

TODAY'S DIARY

What I spent today ☆

Target budget today:
$_____

Food
   Breakfast $_____
   Lunch   _____
   Dinner   _____
   Snacks   _____
Food Total $_____

Entertainment $_____

Shopping $_____

Lodging $_____
Transportation $_____

Other $_____
Total spent today $_____
Over/under budget: $_____

13 14 15 16 17 18 19 20 21 22 23 24 25 26 27 28

My schedule today:

1/ _____

2/ _____

3/ _____

4/ _____

☆

- -

- -

- -

- -

- -

- -

- -

- -

- -

- -

Picture record
Pix #   *Description*

Names, addresses
and places to remember

_____   _____

_____   _____

_____   _____

_____

_____   **Today's thought**

_____   *If you like rainbows, learn to put up*
with a little rain.

Today's checklist

1/ _____

2/ _____

3/ _____

4/ _____

TODAY

Date

Location

Weather

TODAY'S DIARY

_____

_____

_____

_____

_____

_____

_____

_____

_____

_____

What I spent today

Target budget today:
$_____

Food
  Breakfast $_____
  Lunch   _____
  Dinner   _____
  Snacks   _____
Food Total $_____

Entertainment $_____

Shopping $_____

Lodging $_____
Transportation $_____

Other $_____
Total spent today $_____
  Over/under budget: $_____

13 14 15 16 17 18 19 20 21 22 23 24 25 26 27 28

My schedule today:

1/

2/

3/

4/

Picture record

Pix #   *Description*

Names, addresses

and places to remember

Today's thought

The surer you travel the farther you'll go.

Today's checklist

1/_____

2/_____

3/_____

4/_____

TODAY 💼

Date

Location

Weather

TODAY'S DIARY

What I spent today 💼

Target budget today:
$_____

Food
  Breakfast $_____
  Lunch   _____
  Dinner   _____
  Snacks   _____
Food Total $_____

Entertainment $_____

Shopping $_____

Other $_____

Lodging $_____
Transportation $_____

Total spent today $_____
Over/under budget: $_____

13 14 15 16 17 18 19 20 21 22 23 24 25 26 27 28

My schedule today:

1/

2/

3/

4/

Picture record
Pix #   *Description*

Names, addresses
and places to remember

Today's thought

A traveler who has no imagination has no wings.

TODAY

Today's checklist

1/ _____

2/ _____

3/ _____

4/ _____

Date

Location

Weather

TODAY'S DIARY

What I spent today

Target budget today:
$ _____

Food

   Breakfast $_____   Entertainment $_____

   Lunch   _____

   Dinner   _____

   Snacks   _____   Shopping $_____

Food Total $_____

Other $_____

Lodging $_____   Total spent today $_____

Transportation $_____   *Over/under budget:* $_____

13 14 15 16 17 18 19 20 21 22 23 24 25 26 27 28

My schedule today:

1/

2/

3/

4/

Picture record

Pix #   Description

Names, addresses
and places to remember

Today's thought

*Treasure today: what leaves with day's
end can't be returned tomorrow.*

Today's checklist

1/_____

2/_____

3/_____

4/_____

TODAY

Date

Location

Weather

TODAY'S DIARY

_____

_____

_____

_____

_____

_____

_____

_____

_____

_____

What I spent today

Target budget today:
$_____

Food
  Breakfast $_____   Entertainment $_____
  Lunch   _____
  Dinner   _____
  Snacks   _____   Shopping $_____
Food Total $_____

                                        Other $_____
Lodging $_____   Total spent today $_____
Transportation $_____   *Over/under budget:* $_____

13 14 15 16 17 18 19 20 21 22 23 24 25 26 27 28

My schedule today:

1/ _____

2/ _____

3/ _____

4/ _____

Picture record
Pix #   *Description*

_____

_____

_____

_____

_____

_____

_____

Names, addresses
and places to remember

_____

_____

_____

_____

Today's thought

*Keep your eyes open: there's a little
bit of heaven all over the earth.*

TODAY

Today's checklist

1/ _____

2/ _____

3/ _____

4/ _____

Date

Location

Weather

TODAY'S DIARY

What I spent today ☆

Target budget today:

$_____

Food

Breakfast $_____
Lunch _____
Dinner _____
Snacks _____
Food Total $_____

Entertainment $_____

Shopping $_____

Other $_____

Lodging $_____
Transportation $_____

Total spent today $_____
Over/under budget: $_____

13   14   15   16   17   18   19   20   21   22   23   24   25   26   27   28

My schedule today:

1/ _____

2/ _____

3/ _____

4/ _____

Picture record
Pix #   *Description*

_____

_____

_____

_____

_____

_____

_____

Names, addresses
and places to remember

_____

_____

_____

Today's thought

Self-reliance will find a way.

T R I P   D A Y /   1   2   3   4   5   6   7   8   9   10   11   12

Today's checklist
1/ _____

2/ _____

3/ _____

4/ _____

TODAY

Date

Location

Weather

TODAY'S DIARY

What I spent today

Target budget today:

$_____

Food

   Breakfast $_____

   Lunch   _____

   Dinner   _____

   Snacks   _____

Food Total $_____

Entertainment $_____

Shopping $_____

Other $_____

Lodging $_____

Transportation $_____

Total spent today $_____

Over/under budget: $_____

13 14 15 16 17 18 19 20 21 22 23 24 25 26 27 28

My schedule today:

1/

2/

3/

4/

Picture record

Pix #   *Description*

Names, addresses

and places to remember

Today's thought

Starting out is easy. Keeping going is the hard part.

TODAY

Today's checklist

1/_____

2/_____

3/_____

4/_____

Date

Location

Weather

TODAY'S DIARY

What I spent today

Target budget today:
$_____

Food
   Breakfast $_____
   Lunch   _____
   Dinner   _____
   Snacks   _____
Food Total $_____

Entertainment $_____

Shopping $_____

Lodging $_____
Transportation $_____

Other $_____
Total spent today $_____
Over/under budget: $_____

13 14 15 16 17 18 19 20 21 22 23 24 25 26 27 28

My schedule today:

1/ _____

2/ _____

3/ _____

4/ _____

Picture record

Pix #   *Description*

Names, addresses
and places to remember

Today's thought

A new day is a new opportunity.

Today's checklist

1/_____

2/_____

3/_____

4/_____

TODAY

Date

Location

Weather

TODAY'S DIARY

What I spent today

Target budget today:
$_____

Food
   Breakfast $_____
   Lunch   _____
   Dinner   _____
   Snacks   _____
Food Total $_____

Entertainment $_____

Shopping $_____

Other $_____

Lodging $_____
Transportation $_____

Total spent today $_____
Over/under budget: $_____

My schedule today:

1/

2/

3/

4/

Picture record
Pix #   *Description*

Names, addresses
and places to remember

Today's thought

Every day is a new beginning.

Today's checklist

1/ _____

2/ _____

3/ _____

4/ _____

TODAY

Date

Location

Weather

TODAY'S DIARY

What I spent today

Target budget today:
$_____

Food
  Breakfast $_____
  Lunch   _____
  Dinner   _____
  Snacks   _____
Food Total $_____

Entertainment $_____

Shopping $_____

Other $_____
Total spent today $_____
Over/under budget: $_____

Lodging $_____
Transportation $_____

13 14 15 16 17 18 19 20 21 22 23 24 25 26 27 28

My schedule today:

1/

2/

3/

4/

Picture record
Pix #   *Description*

Names, addresses
and places to remember

Today's thought

*The journey sometimes is more excit-
ing than the destination.*

TODAY

Today's checklist

1/_____

2/_____

3/_____

4/_____

Date

Location

Weather

TODAY'S DIARY

What I spent today

Target budget today:

$_____

Food

Breakfast	$_____
Lunch	_____
Dinner	_____
Snacks	_____

Food Total $_____

Lodging $_____
Transportation $_____

Entertainment $_____

Shopping $_____

Other $_____

Total spent today $_____

Over/under budget: $_____

My schedule today:
1/
2/
3/
4/

Picture record
Pix #　　　*Description*

Names, addresses
and places to remember

Today's thought
Some days can be pure heaven.

Today's checklist

1/ _____

2/ _____

3/ _____

4/ _____

TODAY

Date

Location

Weather

TODAY'S DIARY

What I spent today

Food
  Breakfast $_____
  Lunch   _____
  Dinner   _____
  Snacks   _____
Food Total $_____

Lodging $_____
Transportation $_____

Target budget today:
  $_____

Entertainment $_____

Shopping $_____

Other $_____
Total spent today $_____
  Over/under budget: $_____

13 14 15 16 17 18 19 20 21 22 23 24 25 26 27 28

My schedule today:

1/ _____

2/ _____

3/ _____

4/ _____

Picture record

Pix #   *Description*

_____

_____

_____

_____

_____

_____

_____

Names, addresses
and places to remember

_____

_____

_____

Today's thought

Get up at least once to watch the sunrise.

TRIP DAY / 1 2 3 4 5 6 7 8 9 10 11 12

Today's checklist

1/ _____

2/ _____

3/ _____

4/ _____

TODAY

Date

Location

Weather

TODAY'S DIARY

What I spent today

Target budget today:
$_____

Food
  Breakfast $_____
  Lunch   _____
  Dinner   _____
  Snacks   _____
Food Total $_____

Lodging $_____
Transportation $_____

Entertainment $_____

Shopping $_____

Other $_____
Total spent today $_____
  Over/under budget: $_____

13 14 15 16 17 18 19 20 21 22 23 24 25 26 27 28

My schedule today:

1/ _____

2/ _____

3/ _____

4/ _____

Picture record
Pix #   *Description*

_____

_____

_____

_____

_____

_____

_____

Names, addresses
and places to remember

_____

_____

_____

Today's thought

Dreams can ford the deepest river.

Today's checklist

1/_____

2/_____

3/_____

4/_____

TODAY

Date

Location

Weather

TODAY'S DIARY

_____

_____

_____

_____

_____

_____

_____

_____

_____

_____

What I spent today

Target budget today:
$_____

Food

   Breakfast $_____

   Lunch   _____

   Dinner   _____

   Snacks   _____

Food Total $_____

Entertainment $_____

Shopping $_____

Lodging $_____

Transportation $_____

Other $_____

Total spent today $_____

Over/under budget: $_____

My schedule today:

1/

2/

3/

4/

_ _

_ _

_ _

_ _

_ _

_ _

_ _

_ _

Picture record
Pix #   *Description*

Names, addresses
and places to remember

Today's thought

A traveler's train of thought is often only as good as its engineer.

Today's checklist

1/ _____

2/ _____

3/ _____

4/ _____

TODAY 🚢

Date

Location

Weather

TODAY'S DIARY

_____

_____

_____

_____

_____

_____

_____

_____

_____

_____

What I spent today ☆ ☆ ☆

Target budget today:
$_____

Food
  Breakfast $_____
  Lunch   _____
  Dinner   _____
  Snacks   _____
Food Total $_____

Lodging $_____
Transportation $_____

Entertainment $_____

Shopping $_____

Other $_____
Total spent today $_____
  Over/under budget: $_____

13 14 15 16 17 18 19 20 21 22 23 24 25 26 27 28

My schedule today:

1/

2/

3/

4/

Picture record
Pix #   *Description*

Names, addresses
and places to remember

Today's thought

Travel can teach you if you let it.

Today's checklist

1/_____

2/_____

3/_____

4/_____

TODAY

Date

Location

Weather

TODAY'S DIARY

_ _

_ _

_ _

_ _

_ _

_ _

_ _

_ _

What I spent today

Target budget today:
$_____

Food
  Breakfast $_____
  Lunch   _____
  Dinner   _____
  Snacks   _____
Food Total $_____

Lodging $_____
Transportation $_____

Entertainment $_____

Shopping $_____

Other $_____
Total spent today $_____
Over/under budget: $_____

13 14 15 16 17 18 19 20 21 22 23 24 25 26 27 28

My schedule today:

1/ _____

2/ _____

3/ _____

4/ _____

Picture record
Pix #   *Description*

_____

_____

_____

_____

_____

_____

_____

Names, addresses
and places to remember

_____

_____

_____

_____

Today's thought

*Too much of a good thing can be
absolutely wonderful.*

Today's checklist

1/_____

2/_____

3/_____

4/_____

TODAY

Date

Location

Weather

TODAY'S DIARY

_____

_____

_____

_____

_____

_____

_____

_____

_____

_____

What I spent today

Target budget today:
$_____

Food
  Breakfast $_____
  Lunch   _____
  Dinner   _____
  Snacks   _____
Food Total $_____

Entertainment $_____

Shopping $_____

Other $_____

Lodging $_____
Transportation $_____

Total spent today $_____
  Over/under budget: $_____

13 14 15 16 17 18 19 20 21 22 23 24 25 26 27 28

My schedule today:

1/

2/

3/

4/

Picture record
Pix #   *Description*

Names, addresses
and places to remember

Today's thought
Go for excellence, not perfection.

Today's checklist

1/ _____

2/ _____

3/ _____

4/ _____

TODAY

Date

Location

Weather

TODAY'S DIARY

_____

_____

_____

_____

_____

_____

_____

_____

_____

_____

What I spent today

Target budget today:
$_____

Food
  Breakfast $_____
  Lunch   _____
  Dinner   _____
  Snacks   _____
Food Total $_____

Lodging $_____
Transportation $_____

Entertainment $_____

Shopping $_____

Other $_____
Total spent today $_____
Over/under budget: $_____

13 14 15 16 17 18 19 20 21 22 23 24 25 26 27 28

My schedule today:

1/

2/

3/

4/

Picture record

Pix #   *Description*

Names, addresses

and places to remember

Today's thought

If you must economize on something, don't let it be your luxuries.

Today's checklist

1/

2/

3/

4/

TODAY

Date

Location

Weather

TODAY'S DIARY

What I spent today

Food
Breakfast $_____
Lunch
Dinner
Snacks
Food Total $_____

Lodging $_____
Transportation $_____

Target budget today:
$_____

Entertainment $_____

Shopping $_____

Other $_____
Total spent today $_____
Over/under budget: $_____

13 14 15 16 17 18 19 20 21 22 23 24 25 26 27 28

My schedule today:

1/

2/

3/

4/

_ _

_ _

_ _

_ _

_ _

_ _

_ _

_ _

_ _

Picture record

Pix #   *Description*

Names, addresses
and places to remember

Today's thought

You can't enjoy today by dreaming about tomorrow.

Today's checklist

TODAY

1/ _____ Date

2/ _____ Location

3/ _____

4/ _____ Weather

TODAY'S DIARY

What I spent today   *Target budget today:*
$_____

Food
   Breakfast $_____   Entertainment $_____
   Lunch   _____
   Dinner   _____
   Snacks   _____   Shopping $_____
Food Total $_____

                             Other $_____
Lodging $_____   Total spent today $_____
Transportation $_____   *Over/under budget:* $_____

My schedule today:

1/ _____

2/ _____

3/ _____

4/ _____

Picture record

Pix #   *Description*

Names, addresses
and places to remember

Today's thought

*If you like where you are going, the
way is never too hard.*

Today's checklist

TODAY

1/_____ Date

2/_____ Location

3/_____

4/_____ Weather

TODAY'S DIARY

_____

_____

_____

_____

_____

_____

_____

_____

_____

_____

What I spent today

Target budget today:
$_____

Food
  Breakfast $_____   Entertainment $_____
  Lunch   _____
  Dinner   _____
  Snacks   _____   Shopping $_____
Food Total $_____

Other $_____
Lodging $_____   Total spent today $_____
Transportation $_____   *Over/under budget:* $_____

13 14 15 16 17 18 19 20 21 22 23 24 25 26 27 28

My schedule today:

1/ _____

2/ _____

3/ _____

4/ _____

Picture record
Pix #   *Description*

_____
_____
_____
_____
_____
_____
_____

Names, addresses
and places to remember

_____
_____
_____
_____

Today's thought

Travel is rewarding if you learn from it.

Today's checklist

1/ _____

2/ _____

3/ _____

4/ _____

TODAY

Date

Location

Weather

TODAY'S DIARY

_____

_____

_____

_____

_____

_____

_____

_____

_____

_____

What I spent today

Target budget today:
$_____

Food
  Breakfast $_____
  Lunch   _____
  Dinner   _____
  Snacks   _____
Food Total $_____

Entertainment $_____

Shopping $_____

Lodging $_____
Transportation $_____

Other $_____
Total spent today $_____
Over/under budget: $_____

13 14 15 16 17 18 19 20 21 22 23 24 25 26 27 28

My schedule today:

1/

2/

3/

4/

Picture record
Pix #   *Description*

Names, addresses
and places to remember

Today's thought

Nothing can make you feel bad unless you let it.

Today's checklist

TODAY

1/ _____

2/ _____   Date

3/ _____   Location

4/ _____   Weather

TODAY'S DIARY

_____

_____

_____

_____

_____

_____

_____

_____

_____

_____

_____

What I spent today   *Target budget today:*
                                 $_____

Food
   Breakfast $_____   Entertainment $_____
   Lunch   _____
   Dinner   _____
   Snacks   _____   Shopping $_____
Food Total $_____

                                 Other $_____
Lodging $_____   Total spent today $_____
Transportation $_____   *Over/under budget:* $_____

My schedule today:

1/ _____

2/ _____

3/ _____

4/ _____

- -

- -

- -

- -

- -

- -

- -

- -

Picture record		Names, addresses
Pix #	*Description*	*and places to remember*

Today's thought

Money is like fertilizer: useful only when it gets spread around.

Today's checklist

1/ _____

2/ _____

3/ _____

4/ _____

TODAY

Date

Location

Weather

TODAY'S DIARY

What I spent today

Target budget today:
$_____

Food
  Breakfast $_____
  Lunch   _____
  Dinner   _____
  Snacks   _____
Food Total $_____

Entertainment $_____

Shopping $_____

Lodging $_____
Transportation $_____

Other $_____
Total spent today $_____
Over/under budget: $_____

My schedule today:

1/ _____

2/ _____

3/ _____

4/ _____

- -

- -

- -

- -

- -

- -

- -

- -

- -

Picture record		Names, addresses
Pix #	*Description*	*and places to remember*

Today's thought

Two rules for a veteran traveler:
1/ Don't sweat the small stuff and
2/ It's all small stuff.

Today's checklist
1/ _____

2/ _____

3/ _____

4/ _____

TODAY ⊗

Date

Location

Weather

TODAY'S DIARY

_____

_____

_____

_____

_____

_____

_____

_____

_____

_____

What I spent today 💼

Food
  Breakfast $_____
  Lunch   _____
  Dinner   _____
  Snacks   _____
Food Total $_____

Lodging $_____
Transportation $_____

Target budget today:
$_____

Entertainment $_____

Shopping $_____

Other $_____
Total spent today $_____
Over/under budget: $_____

My schedule today:

1/ _____

2/ _____

3/ _____

4/ _____

Picture record

Pix #   *Description*

_____

_____

_____

_____

_____

_____

_____

Names, addresses
and places to remember

_____

_____

Today's thought

*As you travel along in life,
let this be your goal:
Keep your eye upon the donut
and not upon the hole.*

Trip
Notes

----

*It's a good idea to be more under-
standing than you really have to be.*

Part Three

MEMORIES

My final thoughts about this trip

Vacation expense analysis

Special mementoes

Places & things to remember

Ideas for my next trip

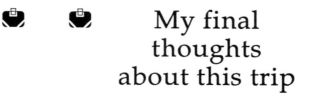

My final thoughts about this trip

Here you can sum up your vacation experiences. For example, did you have a good time? Meet many fine people? Would you recommend the trip to friends or take it again?

My overall comments:

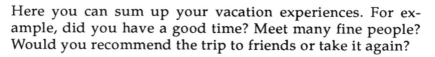

I especially remember these good times:

My worst moments:

What I'd do differently the next time I travel:

_____
_____
_____
_____
_____
_____
_____
_____
_____
_____
_____
_____
_____
_____
_____
_____
_____

On a scale of 1 to 10, I'd rate this vacation a _____

Traveling with hope is sometimes
better than arriving.

Vacation expense analysis

What did you actually spend on your vacation? Here you can figure out your costs to see if you were on budget but also to use as a planning guide for future vacations.

Daily expenses

1/ Total Daily expenses $_____
    (add up your daily *What I spent today* figures)

2/ Other vacation expenses

    Airline or other transportation $ _750. 00_

    Other expenses   _____

                          Total $_____

3/ Analysis

    A/ Total costs of my vacation $_____

    B/ What I planned to spend   _____

    C/ Difference between A & B   _____

4/ Results:

I was _____ *over* _____ *under* my projected costs for my vacation by
                   $_____
4/ I plan to make the following changes financially in my next vacation:

- -

- -

Special mementoes

Here you can keep small personal mementoes of your vacation. Some souvenirs you might want to paste here are ticket stubs to a favorite exhibit or place, a picture postcard or two, small printed programs, or, if you went abroad, some foreign currency samples. You can include a favorite photograph, as well.

*The stars shine most when the moon
is down.*

Special Mementoes / continued

*Happiness is not an absence of
problems but having the ability to deal
with them.*

♣ Places ♣
and things
to remember

Name _____

Address _____

City _____ State _____ Zip _____

Comment: _____

Name _____

Address _____

City _____ State _____ Zip _____

Comment: _____

Name _____

Address _____

City _____ State _____ Zip _____

Comment: _____

Name _____

Address _____

City _____ State _____ Zip _____

Comment: _____

_____

_____

Name _____

Address _____

City _____ State _____ Zip _____

Comment: _____

_____

Name _____

Address _____

City _____ State _____ Zip _____

Comment: _____

_____

Name _____

Address _____

City _____ State _____ Zip _____

Comment: _____

_____

Name _____

Address _____

City _____ State _____ Zip _____

Comment: _____

_____

_____

Ideas
for my
next trip

---

*Sometimes the littlest things
make the biggest difference.*

Trip
notes

Trip
notes

----

*Don't live tomorrow until it actually
arrives.*